WS-ADT-656

D0020202

GUINNESS WORLD RECORDS

GUINNESS
WORLD RECORDS
TM

JUST OUTRAGEOUS!

Extraordinary Records of Unusual Facts & Feats

Collect and Compare with

FEARLESS FEATS:
Incredible Records of Human Achievement

WILD LIVES:
Outrageous Animal & Nature Records

GUINNESS WORLD RECORDS

JUST OUTRAGEOUS!

Extraordinary Records of Unusual Facts & Feats

Compiled by Joanne Mattern & Ryan Herndon

For Guinness World Records:
Laura Barrett, Craig Glenday,
Betty Halvagi, Della Torra Howes

SCHOLASTIC INC.
New York   Toronto   London   Auckland   Sydney
Mexico City   New Delhi   Hong Kong   Buenos Aires

Designed by Michelle Martinez Design, Inc.
Photo Research by Els Rijper
Records from the Archives of Guinness World Records

12 11 10 9 8 7 6 5 4 3 2 1   5 6 7 8 9 10/0

Printed in the U.S.A.

First printing, November 2005

Visit Guinness World Records at www.guinnessworldrecords.com

Contents

A Record-Breaking History

The idea for Guinness World Records grew out of a question. In 1951, Sir Hugh Beaver, the managing director of the Guinness Brewery, wanted to know which was the fastest game bird in Europe — the golden plover or the grouse? Some people argued that it was the grouse. Others claimed it was the plover. A book to settle the debate did not exist until Sir Hugh discovered the knowledgeable twin brothers Norris and Ross McWhirter, who lived in London.

Like their father and grandfather, the McWhirter twins loved information. They were kids just like you when they started clipping interesting facts from newspapers and memorizing important dates in world history. As well as learning the names of every river, mountain range, and nation's capital, they knew the record for pole squatting (196 days in 1954), which language had only one irregular verb (Turkish), and that the grouse — flying at a timed speed of 43.5 miles per hour — is faster than the golden plover at 40.4 miles per hour.

Norris and Ross served in the Royal Navy during World War II, graduated from college, and launched their own fact-finding business called McWhirter Twins, Ltd. They were the perfect people to compile the book of records that Sir Hugh Beaver searched for yet could not find.

The first edition of *The Guinness Book of Records* was published on August 27, 1955, and since then has been published in 37 languages and more than 100 countries. In 2000, the book title changed to *Guinness World Records* and has set an incredible record of its own: Excluding non-copyrighted books, such as the Bible and the Koran, *Guinness World Records* is the best-selling book of all time!

Today, the Keeper of the Records keeps a careful eye on each Guinness World Record, compiling and verifying the greatest the world has to offer — from the fastest and the tallest to the slowest and the smallest, with everything in between.

Is That *Really* True?

For over 50 years, Guinness World Records has been collecting cool facts about the world's most amazing record-breakers. In this collection, we scouted the human, animal, and plant kingdoms and found 50 extraordinary records of unusual facts and feats.

Out of the thousands of incredible records reviewed every year, we have selected these just outrageous record-holders to answer the question: "Is that *really* true?"

Sit down to dinner with a man who eats metal and glass, listen to a concert by the largest animal orchestra, find out about frozen frogs and a frozen man, and try on the largest pair of underwear! These are just a few adventures you can take among the thousands of stories stored in the archives of Guinness World Records.

Yes, that really *is* true!

Chapter 1
The Amazing Human Body

The human body is an amazing creation. One body is the home for thousands of microscopic life-forms, while another body frozen in time gives historians a glimpse at prehistoric life. Some people transform their bodies into pieces of art, using ink and metal. Keep your eyes open to learn unusual facts about your *own* body!

Most Tattooed Man

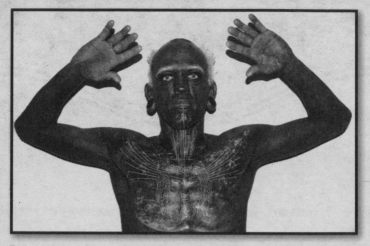

In ancient times, people scratched or poked themselves with sharp bits of bone or pieces of metal, then poured dye into the wounds to create a tattoo. Today, artists use special electric machines with sterilized needles to puncture the skin up to 3,000 times a minute!

Two humans share the artistic-expression record for **Most Tattooed Man**. Tattoos cover an amazing 99.9 percent of their bodies! Lucky Rich is an Australian street performer who had his existing tattoos "blacked over" and added a white design tattooed on top (pictured). Tom Leppard is a retired soldier who lives in Scotland. He's had almost all of his body tattooed with a leopard-skin design. The only parts of his body that are free of tattoos are the insides of his ears and the skin between his toes. See Tom's colorful personality in the special color section of this book.

Most Pierced Woman

Elaine Davidson has more than a few holes in her head . . . and in the rest of her body, too. The **Most Pierced Woman** is from Brazil, South America, and now calls Edinburgh, Scotland, her home, where she runs a Brazilian restaurant. On August 9, 2001, Elaine broke her own record when officials from Guinness World Records counted 720 piercings on her body. Her previous record was 462 piercings during a count in May 2000. At that time, she had 192 piercings on her face alone! The most recent tally is a very shiny 2,520 piercings (pictured)!

Most Successful Parasitic Worm in Humans

It's icky, but true — your body is home to microscopic life-forms, and sometimes even nasty parasites! Lots of different parasites think the human digestive system is a cozy place to call home. The **Most Successful Parasitic Worm in Humans** is a roundworm known as *Ascaris limbricoides* (pictured). This wiggly creature can grow up to 18 inches long and lives in the small intestine. It infects approximately 25 percent of the human population. That's about 1.5 billion people worldwide! Roundworms like lots of company, too. The average victim usually has up to 20 worms in his or her body. Female round-worms can lay about 200,000 eggs per day. That works out to 27 million eggs during a worm's lifetime!

Most Common Skin Infection

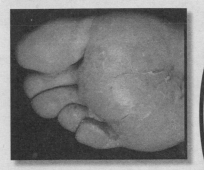

Are your toes dry, red, and really itchy? Then you might have athlete's foot, the **Most Common Skin Infection** in humans (pictured). This condition's scientific name is *Tinea pedis*. It's caused by a fungus that loves to live in damp, warm places. Up to 70 percent of the entire world population has athlete's foot, and most people will get it at least once in their lifetime. Fortunately, doctors have special medicines to kill the fungus and get the feet feeling fit again!

Ancient Illness

The Oldest Known Disease is leprosy. It was first described in ancient Egypt back in 1350 BCE, and is mentioned several times in the Bible. Bacteria attack the skin and nervous system. The first symptom is a patch of skin that loses all feeling. In severe cases, parts of the body, such as the nose and fingers, fall off.

In the past, people infected with this disease were called "lepers," and society shunned them. Many were sent to remote islands or institutions to die untreated because people were afraid of spreading the disease. However, leprosy is not very contagious. Today, antibiotics successfully combat leprosy, and the disease is now 100 percent curable.

Oldest Ice Body

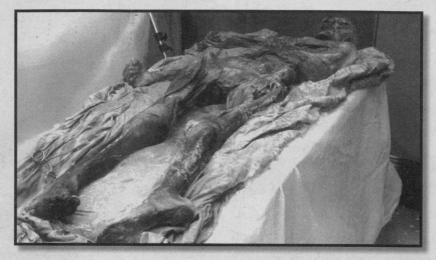

The **Oldest Ice Body** record belongs to Otzi, the oldest man ever found preserved in ice! Otzi lived about 5,300 years ago in the Alps. He was around 40 years old when he died, probably after he was caught in a severe winter storm. Because of the freezing temperatures and heavy snowfall, Otzi's body was protected from predators and decay.

Otzi was found on September 19, 1991, by two German tourists who noticed part of his body sticking out of the snow. Scientists were thrilled at the discovery because it taught them a lot about people who lived during the Neolithic era. Otzi's body was not the only discovery they could study. The ice and snow also preserved Otzi's weapons, a cloak, shoes, and socks made out of soft grass. Today, Otzi is kept in an air-conditioned museum in Italy (pictured).

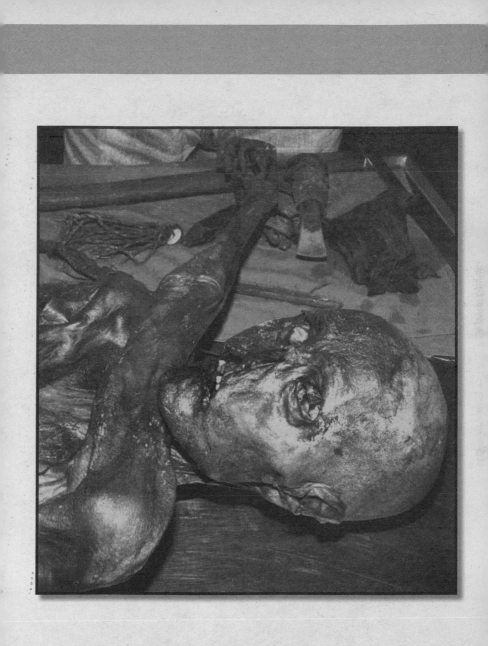

Chapter 2
Picky Eaters

Picky eaters are selective about their diets. But have you ever taken a bite out of an airplane or filled up on mushrooms that cost more than $17,000 a pound? You probably don't shoot your food out of the air with a stream of water like the archerfish does, either. If such strange appetites make you feel queasy, then you may want to skip dessert when reading about the oldest vomit ever found!

Best Aquatic Marksman

Ready, aim, and . . . spit! That's the method used by the **Best Aquatic Marksman**, a fish in Thailand that shoots down its food with its own built-in water pistol! Most fish gobble up other aquatic creatures or swallow bugs floating atop of the water. The archerfish aims for a great meal and rarely misses its mark. Its favorite food lives outside of its water environment. This fish spots an insect or spider sitting on a branch or leaf above the surface, takes aim, then squirts a powerful jet of water out of its mouth, knocking its prey into the water (pictured). Before you can say "Good shot!" the archerfish has finished its meal. The archerfish can squirt water up to five feet.

Most Expensive Edible Fungus

Are you looking for something *really* expensive to eat? Try the white truffle, or *Tuber magnum pico*. It is the world's **Most Expensive Edible Fungus** (pictured). In November 2002, a white truffle sold for $35,000 at a charity truffle auction. The truffle weighed 2 pounds 3 ounces. The buyer was a restaurant owner from Los Angeles, California, who passed the fantastic fungus to his chef for preparation.

White truffles are found only in Piedmont, Emilia-Romagna, Tuscany, and Marches, which are all in Italy. They grow about a foot underground. Pigs and deer naturally track truffles' scent while dogs must be trained to locate this precious fungus.

Strangest Diet

Be careful if Michel Lotito of Grenoble, France, asks you to dinner — you never know what odd things might be on your plate! Lotito is better known as Monsieur Mangetout, the man with the **Strangest Diet**. *Mangetout* is French for "eats everything," and this hungry human really lives up to his name (pictured)! He has been consuming metal and glass since 1959 and is able to eat two pounds of metal per day. His biggest meal was an airplane, but he has also eaten bicycles, TV sets, shopping carts, and even a coffin (with no one inside). Mangetout started eating weird foods when he was nine years old. His stomach lining is twice as thick as an ordinary person's, which allows him to eat pretty much anything he wants without getting sick. Scientists still aren't sure how his body can process metal, glass, and even poisonous materials.

Surprisingly, there are a few foods that make Mr. Mangetout sick. Those foods are bananas and hard-boiled eggs!

Garden Noshers

Certain plants eat animals. These carnivorous plants mostly live in wet places such as rain forests. These places do not have a lot of nitrogen and other nutrients in the soil. Catching bugs and small animals provides the plants with the nutrients they need to survive.

The Largest Carnivorous Plants belong to the *Nepenthacaeae* family. These plants gulp down large frogs, birds, and even rats in the rainforests of Borneo, Indonesia, and Malaysia.

The Venus flytrap, with its underwater cousin the bladderwort plant, shares the record for Fastest Entrapment by a Plant. The "trap" is a leaf. The upper surface of the leaf has hair cells that are extremely sensitive to movement. If an insect lands on the Venus flytrap and triggers two of these cells in a row, the leaf snaps shut and "swallows" its prey in one-tenth of a second! Special enzymes in the plant digest the insect and provide the plant with the nitrogen it needs to grow. In the ocean, meals fall through the hidden trapdoor of the bladderwort plant and are caught in just one-fifth of a second.

Loudest Burp

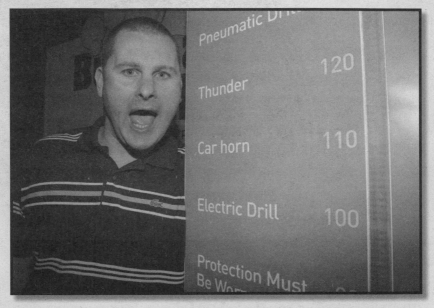

Paul Hunn of the United Kingdom released the world's **Loudest Burp** in the London offices of Guinness World Records on July 20, 2004. Officials measured the burp's sound from 8 feet 2 inches away from Paul (pictured). His burp measured a whopping 104.9 decibels on a certified and calibrated class 1 precision measuring noise-level meter. Paul's secret ingredient: fizzy cola!

A burp is caused by gas inside your body escaping from your stomach. The gas rises up through your esophagus and out through your mouth. Fizzy beverages, such as carbonated sodas, and gassy foods, such as cauliflower or broccoli, can cause big-time burps.

Most Expensive Coffee

A great cup of coffee is the perfect ending to a good meal for many people. But would you spend $300 for a pound of Kopi Luwak, the **Most Expensive Coffee**? Only 500 pounds of this coffee become available every year because its bean collection process is extremely . . . *complicated*. In the mountains of Irian Jaya, Indonesia, the Sumatran civet cat climbs into the coffee trees and eats the ripest coffee cherries. Villagers track the cat and sort through its droppings to find the coffee beans. The crushed beans yield this pricey coffee that has a strong earthy odor with a gooey, chocolaty flavor.

Prehistoric Preservation

History can be made from stomach-churning events. On February 12, 2002, a team of paleontologists led by Professor Peter Doyle of Greenwich University in England announced they had discovered a sample of the Oldest Fossilized Vomit dating back 160 million years (pictured)! The vomit came from a marine reptile called an ichthyosaur that had been found in a quarry in Peterborough, England. This find gave scientists a unique chance to study the feeding habits of these ancient creatures.

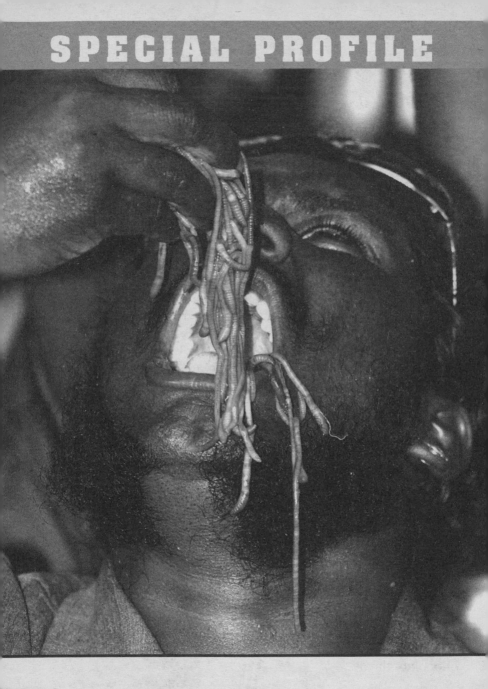

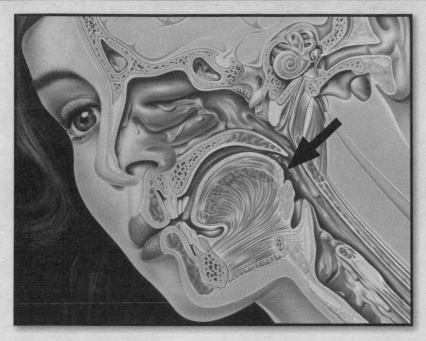

C. Manoharan, better known as "Snake" Manu, likes wiggly creatures and records. "Snake" Manu has many shocking talents besides the one pictured in the color section of this book. On November 15, 2003, he swallowed 200 earthworms in 30 seconds in Chennai City, India. Each worm measured at least four inches long. That meal registered as the **Most Worms Eaten in 30 Seconds** (pictured).

"Snake" Manu can also "snake floss," by feeding small snakes into his mouth and passing them out through his nose! This is possible because there is a space behind the nose and mouth that connect the two sensory organs (see illustration). But don't try this at home!

Chapter 3
The Nose Knows

Are noses good for anything besides smelling and keeping your glasses on your face? Noses are at the center of some just outrageous records. Hold your nose and get up close with a woman whose job it is to make sure you don't stink, a girl who couldn't stop sneezing for almost three years, and the people who *deliberately* create the nastiest odors.

Most Acute Sense of Smell

Bugs let their sense of smell lead them to food, safety, and love! Insects have sensors such as antennae, instead of noses like humans and animals. Among insects, the **Most Acute Sense of Smell** belongs to the male emperor moth (*Eudia pavonia*). By sight, the male moth is a spectacular vision of colors and patterns (pictured). By scent, the female moth is a scene-stealer. According to the results of German experiments carried out in 1961, the chemoreceptors on the male moth's antennae are sensitive enough that it just needs one molecule of the female moth's scent to detect her location, even from 6.8 miles away!

Smelliest Substances

We can't always track down the source of a smell, but chemists can mix up similar odors in laboratories. The **Smelliest Substances** are manmade. "U.S. Government Standard Bathroom Malodor" smells like human feces and was developed to test the effectiveness of deodorants and air fresheners. "Who-Me?" smells like rotting food and corpses. The U.S. government developed such odors in the 1940s, hoping that by making enemy soldiers smell really bad it would embarrass them enough to stop fighting. That plan didn't work, but perhaps it can break up violent crowds or keep warring groups apart.

Nature Stinks!

Certain animals use smell as a natural defense. The skunk sprays its stinky scent if threatened by man or animal. But would you believe a flower smells badly because it wants to attract animals? The *Amorphophallus titanium*, better known by its nickname the "corpse flower," emits the odor of a rotting dead body when in bloom. Its stench attracts scavenger bugs and animals from up to half a mile away. Italian botanist Dr. Oroardo Beccari made the 1878 discovery in the rain forests of Indonesia. The Smelliest Flower grows up to 6.5 feet high and can be seen in the scent-free, color section of this book.

Farthest Marshmallow Nose-Blow

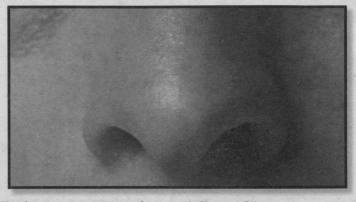

You're not supposed to stick anything up your nose, especially food! The **Farthest Marshmallow Nose-Blow** record of 16 feet 3.5 inches happened on the set of *Guinness World Records: Primetime* in Los Angeles, California, on August 13, 1999. Scott Jeckel of Delavan, Illinois, USA, blew the marshmallow out of his nose and Ray Perisin of Peoria, Illinois, USA, caught it in his mouth.

The two friends discovered their talent when their families were playing cards together. Ray put some popcorn up his nose and laughed. When he did, the popcorn shot across the table. Scott announced that he could shoot popcorn out of his nose farther than Ray could. Then the two moved on to marshmallows, which are more aerodynamic than popcorn.

What does Ray do with the marshmallow after he catches it — he eats it! "I just try not to think about where the marshmallow's being fired from," he says.

WITH STRONG STOMACHS . . .

© JAY/EPA/Landov

PRACTICE MAKES PERFECT

Record attempts require careful planning. "Snake" Manu (real name, C. Manoharan) practices one of his unique talents with a smaller reptile before making his official record attempt. "Snake flossing" calls for a *live cobra* to be inserted into his nose and emerge through his mouth. Read more about "Snake" Manu's wriggly records in "Picky Eaters."

GUINNESS WORLD RECORDS™

AND COLORFUL PERSONALITIES

© Ian Waldie/REX USA

WASH AND WEAR

Clothing fashions go in and out of style every few months. But Tom Leppard spent his clothing allowance, about $7,000, on permanent tattoos that cover almost his entire body. Uncover other sensational feats and facts about "The Amazing Human Body."

GUINNESS WORLD RECORDS™

THESE UNUSUAL MARVELS

Outstink the Worst

CATCHING THE SCENT
Flowers smell in order to attract insects for pollination. The hideous scent of the "corpse flower" drives away everything but certain bugs and animals. Luckily its blooming time only lasts — *phew!* — two days. Sniff out more nasal records in "The Nose Knows."

GUINNESS WORLD RECORDS ™

Frighten More People

© Brian Cassey/AP Wide World Photos

© Art Wolfe/Stone/Getty Images

EEEEK!
Some people run from bugs, but did you know that other people race cockroaches because they are the **Fastest Insects**? Bats hear all the frequencies of a person screeching in fear because they have the **Highest-Frequency Hearing** of any animal. Hear more natural facts in "Wild But True" and then scuttle over to "Bug Out."

Push Farther

© Osman Orsal/AP Wide World Photos

© Neale Haynes/REX USA

Twist Tighter

© Michel Bontemp/PONOPRESSE

A PEOPLE PRETZEL

Some people can easily bend and touch their toes, but Pierre Beauchemin could scratch his ears using his toes! Pierre's nickname was "Mr. Gumby" because he could twist and turn his body as if it was made out of rubber. "Look, No Hands" and "Hair Today" feature other people's unusual talents.

Stretch Wider

Courtesy of Guinness World Records

LOST LAUNDRY?
No, a giant didn't forget his laundry. The Exeter Council for Voluntary Service sewed this humungous pair of cotton underwear, large enough to fit 180 people inside. Stand tall among these oversized record-holders in "G.R.O.S.S.: Great Records of Shocking Size."

GO TO EXTREMES

© Stringer/Reuters

TAKE THE PLUNGE

Marriage is a big step for couples, but some take it to extremes! This couple opted for a private ceremony among the fishes, while 34 other couples bubbled, "I Do," in a mass underwater marriage ceremony. Dive into the details about outrageous group events in "Join Us."

GUINNESS
WORLD RECORDS
TM

...TO BE A GUINNESS WORLD RECORD-HOLDER!

Most Feet and Armpits Sniffed

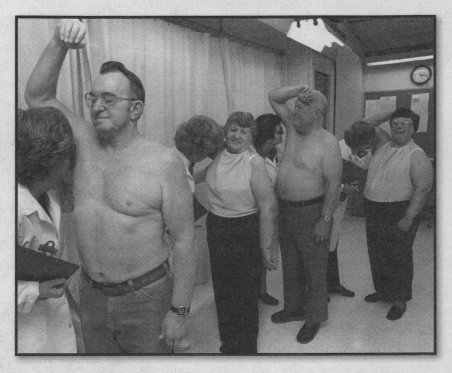

If you think your nose is in tip-top shape, then get in line among the serious sniffers at Hill Top Research Laboratories in Cincinnati, Ohio, USA (pictured). In these labs, the nose truly knows the truth. Hill Top specializes in the testing of odor-reducing products, from soap to soles. After 15 years of being a tester, Madeline Albrecht and her nose broke into the record books with **Most Feet and Armpits Sniffed**. Madeline had sniffed approximately 5,600 feet and thousands of armpits by the year 2000.

Longest Sneezing Fit

What's the most times in a row you've sneezed? Probably two, three times, but Donna Griffiths of Worcestershire, England, sneezed for 978 days straight! On January 13, 1981, twelve-year-old Donna started sneezing (not pictured). At first, Donna sneezed every minute, which means she sneezed an estimated half a million times in the first 365 days of her record. By the last few weeks, however, the sneezes had slowed down to one every five minutes. On September 16, 1983, just as suddenly as she started sneezing, Donna stopped!

Having the **Longest Sneezing Fit** made Donna quite a celebrity. She was featured in newspapers around the world and received handkerchiefs and letters suggesting cures from thousands of well-wishers. Despite all that sneezing, Donna managed to have a normal life. A loyal member of the school swim team, she kept up with her sport in spite of the nasal interruptions. *Achoo!*

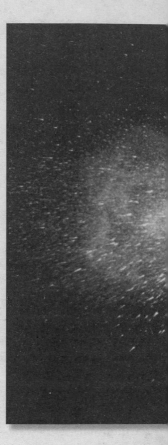

Speed of the Sneeze

Dust, allergies, and cold viruses trigger the nerves inside your nose, with the result being an ah–ah–achoo! Muscles contract and push air out of your nose and mouth, and that's a sneeze!

You may count the number of sneezes, but have you ever clocked the speed of your sneeze? Measuring the Fastest Sneeze means that the airborne particles traveled at 103.6 miles per hour, from the nose here to way over there.

Chapter 4
Hair Today

When these record-holders let down their hair, the world notices! We'll measure the longest ear hair and count the strands behind the story of the hairiest family. Next time you twirl your mustache or braid your tresses, consider just how much care goes into becoming a superhair star!

Longest Ear Hair

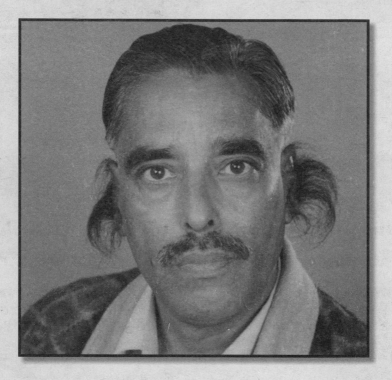

Does longer ear hair improve your hearing? Radhakant Bajpai of Naya Ganj, Uttar Pradesh, India, considers his lengthy locks a special gift. "Making it into *Guinness World Records* is indeed a special occasion for me and my family," he says. Dr. R.P. Gupta measured the sprouting strands coming from the middle of the pinna, or center of Radhakant's outer ears. The medical examiner confirmed the **Longest Ear Hair** length of 5.19 inches at its longest point!

Longest Hair

If you see someone sit on their hair, you probably think their hair is too long. Now picture someone whose hair is more than three times their height! Xie Qiuping from Shenzhen, China, holds the record for the **Longest Hair**. She had stopped cutting her hair in 1973 at age 13.

Xie's hair was 18 feet 5.54 inches long for its official measurement on May 8, 2004. An assistant travels with Xie to help handle her hair. Although Xie says she is used to her hair, she does acknowledge a few changes besides the hair handler. "You need patience, and you need to hold yourself straight when you have hair like this."

Before Xie Qiuping's tremendous tresses set a world record, the hair record took root in another family. A medicine man named Hoo Sateow from Chang Mai, Thailand, had his last haircut in 1929 at age 18. When he fell ill afterward, Hoo decided never to cut his hair again.

On November 21, 1997, Hoo's hair measured 16 feet 11 inches long. A few inches longer than Yee, his brother, whose long locks measured 16 feet long! Hoo weaves his long locks into a beehive shape and tucks it under a hat to keep it out of the way. Villagers aid the brothers in their monthly hair care maintenance.

Longest Mustache

Before growing a full beard, many men start with a mustache. Ram Singh Chauhan believes that someday he will be in the record books with his mustache (pictured). Yet he falls short at only 6 feet 5 inches. The current record-holder, Kalyan Ramji Sain, of India, started letting his mustache grow out in 1976. In July 1993, his mustache had reached a record-setting span of 11 feet 1 inch. Although he did tend to the **Longest Mustache**, the right side measured 5 feet 7 inches, but the left side was only 5 feet 6 inches.

Longest Beard on a Living Male

If the mustache just isn't enough, then it's time for the full facial treatment! Shamsher Singh of Punjab, India, knew his beard was long, but on August 18, 1997, he learned its official measurements. From the end of his chin to the tip of the beard's lengthiest whisker, Shamsher's beard measured 6 feet long, making it the **Longest Beard on a Living Male** (pictured). Yet Hans Langseth of Kensett, Iowa, USA, still had the **Longest Beard Ever** at an amazing 17 feet 6 inches, measured upon his death in 1927. In 1967, Hans' beard was presented to the Smithsonian Institution in Washington, DC, making it another unusual piece of American history!

Hairiest Family

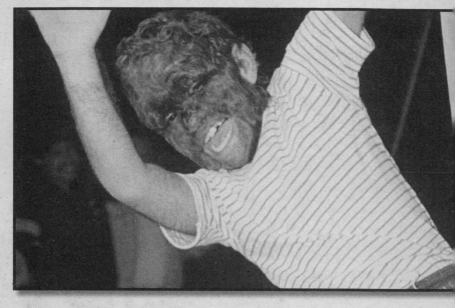

Victor "Larry" and Gabriel "Danny" Ramos Gomez from Mexico are two of 19 members, spanning five generations, of the **Hairiest Family** (pictured). The brothers are circus performers, jumping on trampolines and swinging on the trapeze. But what makes them even more unique is the dark, thick hair that covers 98 percent of their bodies.

There is a medical condition called hypertrichosis, also known as werewolf syndrome. Women are covered with a light to medium coat of excessive facial and torso hair, while men have darker and thicker hair. All the Ramos Gomez clan were born with this condition, and are happy with their hairy selves.

Your hair is constantly falling out and being replaced by new growth. The average person loses 100 hairs a day. At any given time, 90 percent of your hair is growing.

- But do blonds have more fun? They have more hair per inch to enjoy it with! An average blond has 140,000 hairs on his or her head.

- Brunettes have an average of 110,000 hairs per head.

- Then come black-haired people, who have 105,000 hairs apiece.

- Redheads have the fewest hairs — only 90,000 on the average redhead. . . .

The family assisted scientists with the analysis of their genes. Significant evidence linked the condition with the long arm of the X chromosome. Larry and Danny don't care about the reason behind their appearance. Larry says, "I'd never cut the hair off. I'm very proud to be who I am."

Chapter 5
Look! No Hands!

Just how far will people push their own body's natural talents to become a Guinness World Record-breaker? See the most active muscle get a workout by squirting milk and popping from its sockets. Watch "Mr. Gumby" twist and turn his entire body into more shapes than a pretzel. Teach your feet the technique of making the perfect sandwich. Remember, the only hands involved here are the ones turning the page!

Farthest Ear Slingshot

If you think wiggling your ears is extraordinary, check out this "ear-ie" record by Monte Pierce of Bowling Green, Kentucky, USA. On October 29, 1999, Monte propelled a dime from his flexible earlobes a total distance of 10 feet 10.5 inches. The record for **Farthest Ear Slingshot** was set in the Los Angeles, California, studio of the *Guinness World Records: Primetime* TV show. Naturally, Monte holds the matching record for **Longest Stretched Earlobes** (pictured). Monte began pulling on his ears as a child to ease pressure caused by earaches. At age 18, officials declared his earlobes the longest at 2.54 inches, able to touch under his chin. Doctors determined his hearing is unaffected by his stretchy practice.

Farthest Milk Squirting Distance

People squirt milk out of their mouth or nose, but usually not on purpose. How about a man squirting milk out of his eye whenever he wants? On August 31, 2004, Ilker Yilmaz earned the record for **Farthest Milk Squirting Distance** when he snorted milk up his nose and then squirted it 9.2 feet out of his left eye.

The eye squirting is possible because of an oddly shaped tear duct that created a pressure leak inside his eyelids. Ilker first noticed something unusual when he saw bubbles coming out of his left eye during an underwater swim. Once he understood his talent, he practiced for three years and with more than 100 liters of milk to perfect his technique. Get an eyeful of Ilker in the special color section of this book.

Keeping Active

The Most Active Muscles in the human body are found not in the legs or arms, but in the eyes. Scientists think that the eye muscles move more than 100,000 times a day. That's a lot of looking around! Even more incredible is that most of these movements take place during sleep. When you dream, you are in a period of sleep known as REM. Appropriately enough, REM stands for Rapid Eye Movement!

Farthest Eyeball Popper

Have you ever felt as if your eyes popped out of your head? Kimberly Goodman of Chicago, Illinois, USA, can do this trick on cue!

Kimberly discovered her quirky talent in 1992 by accident, luckily not a serious one. She hit one of her eyes while taking off a Halloween mask and — *POP!* — her eyeball came out of its socket. Kimberly popped her eyeball back into its rightful place, much to the astonishment of her friends, and since that day has practiced her oddball talent. Over the years, she learned to pop them out voluntarily, and can pop out one eyeball or both at the same time. Her secret: "I sort of squint, pull my eyelid back, and out it comes." Although Kim hasn't visited any eye doctors, her perfect vision has not been affected by hours of popping practice.

On June 13, 1998, Kimberly made her mark during the television show *Guinness World Records: Primetime.* The young woman's eyeballs protruded 0.43 inches beyond her eye sockets to earn her a place in the record books as the **Farthest Eyeball Popper**.

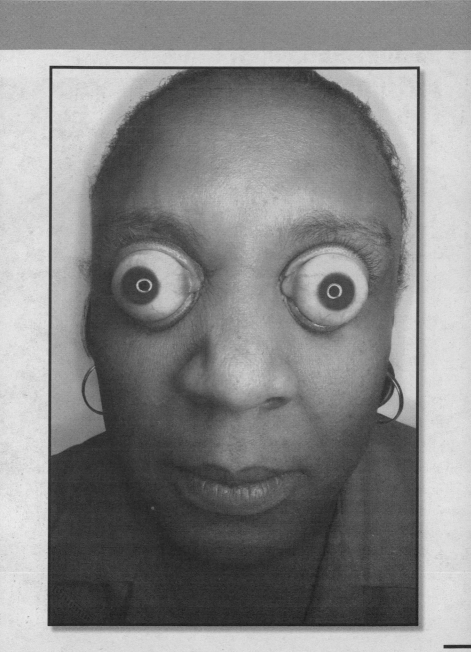

Fastest Sandwich Made by Human Feet

Rob Williams of Austin, Texas, USA, demonstrated his unusual sandwich-making skills on November 10, 2000, during the TV show *Guinness World Records: Primetime*. He made a bologna-and-cheese sandwich in 1 minute 57 seconds . . . using only his feet! Rob is a member of the comedy and juggling group, The Flaming Idiots. Among their fire-based tricks is Rob's popular **Fastest Sandwich Made by Human Feet** (pictured). Ingredients needed are: two slices of bread removed from the package, bologna (without the rind), slices of processed cheese (neatly unwrapped), lettuce, tomato slices, mustard, mayonnaise, and sliced pickles. "It's a pretty good sandwich, if you can get over the way it was created," Rob claims. Wash your feet before and after you eat!

Use Your Head

When somebody says, "Use your head," they mean to think before doing something. In the case of Leonardo D'Andrea of Italy, he uses his head for more than thinking through his next record attempt. On September 11, 2004, Leonardo smashed his previous record for Most Watermelons Crushed when he split 22 watermelons into pieces just by using his head in the 1-minute time limit. The feat was performed on the set of *Guinness World Records: 50 Years, 50 Records* in London, England.

Most Elastic Man

After you've perfected your sandwich-making technique, how about scratching your ears with your feet? Pierre Beauchemin could do this trick, and much more. He was so flexible that he became known as "Mr. Gumby." *Guinness World Records* first listed him as the world's **Most Elastic Man** in 1983.

Pierre's parents discovered his talent when he was one year old. Pierre could twist his arms and legs in outrageously contorted positions (pictured). He could even turn his legs completely around to walk backward. One time, he folded himself down small enough to fit inside a picnic basket! Flip over to the color section for a glimpse of Pierre's unique breakfast style.

Pierre performed these tricks by dislocating his joints and stretching his muscles. Doctors were alarmed by his twisting and turning, and said he would be completely disabled by the time he was 30 years old. They were wrong. Pierre continued displaying his contortionist talent for amazed audiences around the world, until his death on November 4, 2000.

Chapter 6
Join Us

Individuals act differently when part of a crowd. Throwing tomatoes is not considered good behavior,—unless it's during a famous annual food fight among thousands of cheering participants. Weddings are private ceremonies, —unless 20 other couples strap on scuba gear for an underwater marriage celebration. Set your fears aside and join the fun with these mass-participation record-holders.

Most Couples Married Underwater Simultaneously

Ready to dive into marriage? In 2001, on February 14 (Valentine's Day, of course!), 34 couples from 22 different countries joined together to become the **Most Couples Married Underwater Simultaneously!** The couples dove 32.8 feet near Kradan Island, Southern Thailand, for the wettest ceremony. The Trang Chamber of Commerce and Thai Ariways International organized the event for publicity of Kradan Island. Everyone received waterproof marriage certificates. Then each couple took off their mouthpieces to share an underwater kiss! Check out the special color section of this book for a ceremony in the deep blue sea.

Most People Fire Breathing Simultaneously

A record that definitely can't be set underwater is **Most People Fire Breathing Simultaneously**! On September 6, 2004, a total 70 fire breathers gathered near the legendary Stonehenge in Wilshire, UK, to light up the sky as the sun set (pictured). The fiery event was filmed by Granada Television for the TV show, *Guinness World Records: 50 Years, 50 Records*.

Fire breathing is extremely dangerous, both to the performer and onlookers. This trick falls under the category of "Do Not Try This at Home!" Trained jugglers and circus performers learn to manipulate special torches, fuel, and breathing techniques to control the flames and avoid inhaling fire into their lungs. First they practice with unlit torches. Then they work with one lit torch, adding more torches as they gain more skill.

Most People Simultaneously "Slimed"

Getting "slimed" has become an honorable rite of passage during Nickelodeon's TV shows. Superstars from music, movies (like Will Ferrell, pictured), and even Guinness World Record-breakers get slimed in front of cheering crowds during Nickelodeon's annual Kids' Choice Awards. The slime-perfect location for the **Most People Simultaneously "Slimed"** record was also during Nickelodeon's *Slime Time Live* show. The event used approximately 150 gallons of green slime to dump upon 762 people on October 27, 2003, at Universal Studios in Orlando, Florida, USA.

Largest Annual Food Fight

The post-lunch cleanup of your school cafeteria can't compare to the town of Buñol, Spain! Every August since 1944, Buñol hosts a tomato festival called the Tomatina. The weeklong festival honors Saint Louis, the town's patron saint, with bonfires, fireworks, and entertainment. On the last day of the festival, trucks unload their cargo of tomatoes onto the crowded streets. People scoop up their organic ammunition and the **Largest Annual Food Fight** begins! Soon the crowds are drenched in tomato paste (pictured on the front cover). Red rivers of juice, 12 inches deep, flow along the streets. How did this wild food fight become a tradition? Some say a few boys became bored and began throwing tomatoes. Others claim a cart, carrying tomatoes, tipped over in the town square. Whatever its origin, the Tomatina creates a record-breaking mess! In 1999, the Tomatina hit a milestone — *splat!* — after 25,000 people spent an hour throwing a total sum of 275,500 pounds of tomatoes.

Largest Garlic Festival

Every year, at least 130,000 people attend the **Largest Garlic Festival** in honor of the tasty, yet stinky, herb (pictured). The three-day Gilroy Garlic Festival takes place in Gilroy, California, USA. The festival starts with the lighting of a 25-foot fake bulb of garlic. Participants then sample a wide range of garlic-flavored food — everything from meat to ice cream! The Gilroy Garlic Festival started in 1979. By the year 2000, organizers estimated that more than two million people had attended the fragrant feast. Do you wonder if organizers give out breath mints, too?

The Stinking Rose

The pungent herb known as garlic, or the stinking rose, has had a long and flavorful history. The ancient Egyptians worshipped garlic. Greek Olympians chewed it to gain strength for their athletic feats. Legends also say that garlic can keep vampires away.

Most people don't use garlic to chase away vampires. Instead, it is a popular spice for cooking. Garlic can be added to sauces, spread on bread, and mixed with pasta. Garlic is even good for you! Scientists have discovered that garlic can kill bacteria, keep your heart healthy, and even keep cold germs away.

What makes garlic so powerful? It includes a chemical called allicin. Allicin is able to block certain organisms that cause infection and illness. Unfortunately, allicin is also responsible for garlic's powerful smell!

Chapter 7
Good Sports

Everyone is familiar with such popular sports as baseball, football, and soccer. But have you heard about the demands of bog snorkeling or toe wrestling? Those are two selections of the just outrageous sports records coming up, plus the world championships with the heaviest participants. (No, it isn't sumo wrestling!) So, let's get physical!

Most Consecutive Bog Snorkeling World Championships

Bogs are like swamps, and plentiful in the United Kingdom, as is the sport of bog snorkeling (pictured). Wearing snorkels and flippers, 93 entrants in the World Championships swam two complete lengths of a 60-yard trench cut through the Waen Rhydd peat bog on August 26, 2002. Philip John, only 15-years-old, won that race in a blistering 1 minute 35 seconds. He has taken home the coveted award twice, for 2002 and 2004. Yet Steve Griffiths from the UK holds the record for the **Most Consecutive Bog Snorkeling World Championships**. Steve has won the championships three times consecutively, from 1985 to 1987.

Fastest Butt Boarding

Skateboarders used to sit down on their boards when a hill was too steep to ride in a standard position. Before you knew it, skaters were laying down a new speed sport, and extreme sports enthusiasts flocked to the hills.

Darren Lott moved from street luge into buttboard racing (pictured). He clocked in at 65.24 miles per hour for **Fastest Butt Boarding** in Fountain Hills, Arizona, USA, on September 26, 1998.

A man of many talents, Darren is a qualified diving instructor, an accomplished rock climber, a motocross driver, a fifth-degree black belt in Kung Fu San Soo, and a movie fight scene choreographer.

Made of wood and only 4 feet long, a buttboard is basically a skateboard — a board and four wheels — for your body. Boarders must wear helmets and protective clothing, and can participate in organized races with street permits and hay bales padding the sharp turns.

Fastest Wife Carrying Champion

The World Wife Carrying Championships have been held every year since 1992 in Sonkajarvi, Finland. Competitors carry a woman through an obstacle course of log hurdles, hairpin turns, and a water hazard. Partners don't have to be married (unless competing in the "classic" category), but women must be over 17 years old and wear a crash helmet during the race. If the husband drops his wife, the team is given a 15-second penalty.

While many competitors carry the wife piggyback, Estonians flip the wife upside down so her legs dangle over the husband's chest. This allows the man's arms to move more freely, which means he can run faster (pictured). The **Fastest Wife Carrying Champion** is Margo Uusorg for hefting Birgit Ulricht of Läänernaa, Estonia, through the 771-foot obstacle course in just 55.5 seconds on July 1, 2000.

Most Toe Wrestling World Championships

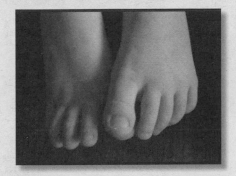

Every year, the Toe Wrestling World Championships are held on the first Saturday in June at Ye Olde Royal Oak in Wetton, England. The **Most Toe Wrestling World Championships** title for men belongs to Alan Nash of England. Nash — whose nickname is "Nasty" — has won five times, in 1994, 1996, 1997, 2000, and 2002. Karen Davies, also of England, holds the women's title as a four-time champion between 1999 and 2002. Get a close-up view of the sport in the special color section of this book.

Toe Tips

The idea behind toe wrestling debuted at Ye Olde Royal Oak in 1976.

The rules are simple, yet taxing on the foot muscles: Wrestlers compete barefoot. Men always compete against men, and women against women. Opponents lock toes and — on the command "Toes away!" — attempt to "toe-down" their opponent by forcing his or her toes across the specially constructed ring, known as a "toe-rack." Toe-riffic winners take the best of three matches.

World Championships with the Heaviest Athletes

Are you ready for a thunderous polo match? Although this fast-paced sport is usually played on horseback, the World Elephant Polo Association (WEPA) plays on — you guessed it — the backs of elephants!

This organization has hosted a pachyderm polo tournament every December, beginning in 1982, played on a grass airfield in Megauly, Nepal. Four riders form a team, with a riding pair steering each elephant.

The elephants are the star players of the **World Championships with the Heaviest Athletes** (pictured). Adult male Asian elephants can weigh more than 11,000 pounds, and there are no weight restrictions. These athletes must follow one important rule while playing — they are not allowed to lie down in front of the goal.

Chapter 8
Wild But True

People shock others with their quirky talents, but animals also have extraordinary talents and stories to surprise us. Hunt alongside a mammal that sees with its ears. Chill out in a deep freeze with a frog. Curl up in the largest nest. So keep your fur on — it's time to explore the animal world, starting with the wildest casting call.

Largest Assemblage of Animals in a Film

Casting the perfect actor for a movie role takes a lot of patience, and sometimes an animal wrangler! The original version of *Around the World in Eighty Days* (1956) required the **Largest Assemblage of Animals in a Film**. Director Daniel Anderson helmed the story of a global explorer named Phileas Fogg, played by David Niven, who met many different people — and animals — in his big screen adventure. The casting sheet swelled to a total of 8,552 animals: 3,800 sheep, 2,448 buffalo, 950 donkeys, 800 horses, 512 monkeys, 17 bulls, 15 elephants, 6 skunks, and 4 ostriches (including this ostrich in action, pictured).

Highest-Frequency Hearing

Bats suffer from poor eyesight, but having the **Highest-Frequency Hearing** makes them accurate hunters of bugs and fruit, day or night. A high-pitched series of clicks and chirps, called ultrasonic echolocation, guide bats on their way through the world. Most bat species use frequencies in the 20–80 kilohertz range, but some can hear frequencies as high as 120–250 kilohertz. Humans, by comparison, can hear only up to about 20 kilohertz. Hang out with these flying hunters in the special color section of this book.

Echo Where? There!

Echolocation is a method of sensory perception. Animals such as bats and whales use echolocation to orient themselves to their surroundings, detect obstacles, communicate with others, and find food.

How does echolocation work? The animal sends out sound waves through its mouth or nose. When the sound waves hit an object, an echo comes back and the animal can "see" what they are hearing. A bat's sonar system is so accurate that it can detect insects as tiny as a gnat and objects as fine as a human hair!

Largest Colony of Mammals

Some cities are crowded with millions of people. But a prairie dog colony in North America has most big cities beat in population numbers. The black-tailed prairie dog, which belongs to the family Sciuridae, lives in the western USA and northern Mexico. This rodent is known for its large colonies (pictured). In 1901, a prairie dog colony was uncovered that contained about *400 million* individuals. The **Largest Colony of Mammals** covered 23,705 square miles. That's almost the size of Ireland!

Most Cold Resistant Animal

Frogs are cold-blooded animals, which means that their body temperature is the same temperature as their environment. Therefore, most frogs freeze to death if the temperature drops below 32°F. Yet surprisingly, the **Most Cold Resistant Animal** is a frog (pictured)!

North of the Arctic Circle is a habitat of the woodland frog (*Rana sylvatica*). Its blood contains glucose, a type of sugar, which acts as antifreeze in the frog's vital organs. Up to 65 percent of the water in the frog's body can freeze without causing damage to the frog's cells. Once the outside temperature warms up, the frog thaws out and hops away, none the worse for its long winter nap.

Largest Mammal to Build a Nest

Birds are not the only nest-building animals in the world. Certain mammals construct nests as their home. The gorilla (*Gorilla gorilla*) of Africa is the **Largest Mammal to Build a Nest** (pictured). Adult male gorillas are big — between 5.5 feet to 6.5 tall, weighing between 300–500 pounds. So they require a large, roomy nest. Every day, these gorillas create new ground nests from leaves, branches, and other vegetation. These huge, round nests can measure more than 3 feet in diameter.

Nesters

The African gorilla builds its nests on the ground. Other smaller gorilla species build nests high in the trees. These nests are built where branches fork for extra support. Each gorilla has its own nest, except for mothers and their babies who share a nest. Often gorillas make a nest during the day to rest in, then make a different nest to sleep in at night. Each nest is used only once.

Birds are the most commonly known nest builders. Who holds the record for the Largest Bird's Nest? The bald eagle (*Haliaeetus leucocephalus*). In 1963, a bald eagle nest near St. Petersburg, Florida, USA, measured 9 feet 6 inches wide and 20 feet deep. It weighed more than two tons! Bald eagle nests can get heavy because the birds add sticks to them every year.

Chapter 9
Bug Out

Insects set all sorts of records without holding any organized competitions . . . until those nosy humans get involved. Whether scuttling the fastest or web-spinning the longest, these creepy-crawlies do what they do naturally while we pull out stopwatches and measuring tape. Put that bug spray away and wipe off your magnifying glass for a closer look at a bug's life.

Largest Continuous Areas of Spiderwebs

Since primitive times people have used spider silk for netting to carry arrows and fish, and even for clothing. Although these thin strands look flimsy, the webbing is in fact strong enough to snag and trap a spider's daily meals, from insects to mice. Luckily for us, there aren't gigantic spiderwebs out there to catch humans . . . right? Spiders of the Indian genus *Stegodyphus*—who build intricate webs of three-dimensional depths, with strands interweaving and overlapping everything in their path—hold the record for the **Largest Continuous Areas of Spiderwebs** (pictured). Their webs can cocoon vegetation in a silken mass for several miles.

Largest Wasp Nest

Remember the previous record-holders in building nests? Wasps also build nests. Their fortresslike homes are constructed out of wood pulp. The insect collects fiber strands from wooden fences, telephone poles, and even cardboard. It flies back to its chosen location and begins chewing. Mixing wood fiber with saliva creates a paste that the wasp uses to coat the nest structure. The dried paste becomes a tough paper shell, able to withstand wind, rain, but not curious people. Yoichiro Kawamura of Japan discovered the **Largest Wasp Nest** in Yonegaoka, Japan (pictured). The nest weighed 17 pounds 8 ounces, with a circumference of 8 feet, and was measured on May 18, 1999.

Fastest-Moving Insect

We know how quickly bugs can move, especially when we're chasing them. Next time you see a cockroach scuttle by, grab a stopwatch instead of a broom. Perhaps the next racing champion is stabled beneath your sink. The **Fastest-Moving Insect** record belongs to *Periplaneta americana*, a large tropical cockroach of the order Dictyoptera. The insect was clocked at 3.36 miles per hour in 1991 at the University of California at Berkeley, California, USA. That works out to moving 50 body lengths per second! Racing enthusiasts replaced binocular with magnifying glasses and downsized racetracks in various international locales (pictured). See a pet racing cockroach and his owner in the special color section of this book.

Races for the Roaches

Jet over to the land Down Under, home to 450 native species of cockroach. Brisbane, Australia, hosts the annual Cockroach Races in January, which marked their 23rd year in 2005 with 7,000 humans participating in the fund-raiser for a local children's hospital. Racing roaches scuttle around a circular track or compete in a steeplechase, challenged by a garden hose blocking the finish line.

Handlers should visit the Bug Bowl in April, an annual celebration of creepy-crawlies hosted by the Department of Entomology at Purdue University, Indiana, USA. After 15 years, attendance has swelled to 45,000 people milling around the roach racetrack, bug petting pen, and cricket-spitting contest. The next hot roach sport? Harness racing!

Greediest Animal

Breakfast is the most important meal of the day, especially if you are a freshly hatched caterpillar and the **Greediest Animal** in the record books (pictured). The North American polyphemus moth (*Antheraea polyphemus*) lays 3 to 5 eggs on a leaf and flies off. When the caterpillar hatches, it begins chowing down on its eggshell. The larva consumes an amount equal to 86,000 times its own birthweight in the first 56 days of its life. In human terms, this would be equivalent to a 7-pound baby eating 273 tons of food!

Largest Colony of Ants

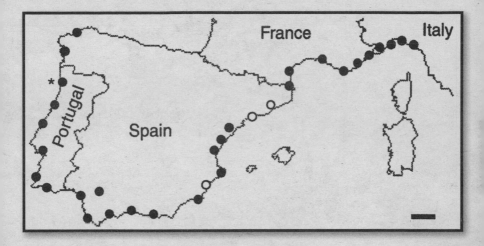

The **Largest Colony of Ants** stretches 3,700 miles and spans four countries, from northern Italy, through the south of France to the Atlantic coast of Spain and Portugal (see black dots on map). This super colony was unearthed by a group of Swiss, French, and Danish scientists. The colony itself contains billions of a related species of Argentine ant, *Linepithema humile*, introduced into Europe over 80 years ago. Ants have a complex society, which is ruled by a queen. Normally ants battle rival nests, yet this super colony's residents recognize and cooperate with each other, even if they come from opposite ends of the colony!

Chapter 10
G.R.O.S.S.

Some records are gross. Others are G.R.O.S.S.!
Those letters stand for Great Records of
Shocking Size. Nature and humans can
perform feats so outrageous and in such
an oversized way that only Guinness World
Records can measure the results. From
making a large fashion statement to sitting
in on a rare performance by a pachyderm
orchestra, these gigantic record-holders will
shock you with their size!

Largest Underwear

Flip to the special section of this book to see the **Largest Underwear** in full color!

Who is responsible for this supersized fashion statement? On June 7, 2003, the Exeter Council for Voluntary Service in England revealed the world's largest pair of cotton underwear at the County Rugby Ground. Just how big were these pants? They measured 31.29 feet wide and 16 feet tall. Paul Bunyan, please call your tailor!

In celebration of the record-breaking feat, 180 people crammed into the undies. "It's fantastic to break a world record," said Simon Langridge, who helped make the underwear. "This is a reward for all the hard work that's been put into this record attempt."

The Exeter Council was not the first group to think of making really big underpants. The record was previously held by Bartle Bogie Hegarty Ltd. and Cunning Stunts for a British magazine promotion. That pair of shorts fell short at 14 feet by 28 feet 7 inches.

Largest Shoes

A snappy pair of pants needs a matching set of shoes. Head down to Marikina City, in the Philippines, for footwear in a size 753! That's the foot size fit by a pair of 125-foot-long shoes built on October 21, 2002. The appropriately named Marikina Colossal Footwear Team created the **Largest Shoes** (pictured). The pair of footwear required more than 800 feet of leather, plus 50 buckets of glue, and more than 1,000 yards of thread. It took 20,000 stitches to assemble the shoes, which were the equivalent of 250 normal-size shoes. Is that little old lady looking for a new shoe to call home? She and 30 of her closest friends can live in one of these shoes!

Biggest Flower

Here's a flower straight from a giant's garden! *Rafflesia arnoldii* is the **Biggest Flower**. Each bloom measures 35.8 inches wide and can weigh up to 24.3 pounds. The flower's petals are 0.75 inches thick. *Rafflesia* grows in the rain forests of Southeast Asia, where plants can get quite large because of the hot weather and steady rain. This orange, brown, and white flower is actually a parasite that attaches itself to vines and feeds off of other plants. There are 16 known species of this giant flower. It was named after the two scientists who discovered it, Dr. Stamford Raffles and Dr. Joseph Arnold.

Largest Animal Brain

The star of the classic book *Moby Dick* also carries the **Largest Animal Brain** inside its enormous skull (pictured). The sperm whale (*Physeter macrocephalus*) grows between 40 to 65 feet long and swims wherever it pleases, except for the chilly polar areas. The whale's name comes from the spermaceti organ in their heads, responsible for producing the waxy oil sought after by whale hunters. The sperm whale's brain weighs approximately 19 pounds 13 ounces. Let's take out the scales and compare some brains: A bull African elephant's brain·can reach up to 11 pounds 14 ounces, while a human brain weighs, on average, 3 pounds.

Largest Animal Orchestra with the Most Members

In 2000, Americans Richard Lair and David Soldier came up with a unique idea to promote the conservation of the endangered Asiatic elephant. They created the 12-piece Thai Elephant Orchestra, also known as the **Largest Animal Orchestra with the Most Members** (pictured). All the elephants in the orchestra are between 7 and 18 years old. They improvise their own music on a variety of percussion and wind instruments. Audiences can attend their concerts at the Thai Elephant Conservation Center in Lampang, Thailand. Although there are no plans to tour, the orchestra's unique music is available on CD with a second album, *Elephant Rhapsodies*, on the way.

BE A
Record-Breaker!

Message from the Keeper of the Records: Record-breakers are the ultimate in one way or another — the youngest, the oldest, the tallest, the smallest. So how do you get to be a record-breaker? Follow these important steps:

1. Before you attempt your record, check with us to make sure your record is suitable and safe. Get your parents' permission. Next, contact one of our officials by using the record application form at *www.guinnessworldrecords.com*.

2. Tell us about your idea. Give us as much information as you can, including what the record is, when you want to attempt it, where you'll be doing it, and other relevant information.

a) We will tell you if a record already exists, what safety guidelines you must follow during your attempt to break that record, and what evidence we need as proof that you completed your attempt.

b) If your idea is a brand-new record nobody has set yet, we need to make sure it meets our requirements. If it does, then we'll write official rules and safety guidelines specific to that record idea and make sure all attempts are made in the same way.

3. Whether it is a new or existing record, we will send you the guidelines for your selected record. Once you receive these, you can make your attempt at any time. You do not need a Guinness World Record official at your attempt. But you do need to gather evidence. Find out more about the kind of evidence we need to see by visiting our website.

4. Think you've already set or broken a record? Put all of your evidence as specified by the guidelines in an envelope and mail it to us at Guinness World Records.

5. Our officials will investigate your claim fully — a process that can take a few weeks, depending on the number of claims we've received and how complex your record is.

6. If you're successful, you will receive an official certificate that says you are now a Guinness World Record-holder!

Need more info? Check out the Kids' Zone on *www.guinnessworldrecords.com* for lots more hints and tips and some top record ideas that you can try at home or at school. Good luck!

Photo Credits

The publisher would like to thank the following for their
kind permission to use their photographs in this book:

6 Lucky Rich © Guinness World Records; 7 Elaine Davidson © Nils Jorgensen/Rex
Features; 8 Roundworm © CNRI/Photo Researchers, Inc.; 9 Athlete's Foot © Dr. P.
Marazzi/Photo Researchers, Inc.; 10 Otzi - 1 © Simone Crepaldi/AP Wide World
Photos; 11 Otzi - 2 © Werner Nosko/Reuters/Landov; 14 Archerfish © G. I. Bernard/
Photo Researchers, Inc.; 15 White Truffle © Owen Franken/CORBIS; 16 Monsieur
Mangetout © Michael Lotito/Rex Features; 18 Paul Hunn © Ray Tang/Rex Features;
19 Oldest Vomit courtesy of University of Greenwich; 20 C. Manoharan © Stringer/
India/Reuters; 21 Nose-Throat Illustration © John Bavosi/Photo Researchers, Inc.; 24
Emperor Moth © Paul Hobson/Photo Researchers, Inc.; 25-26 Laboratory, Skunk,
Nose © Photodisc via SODA; 27 Hill Top Research Labs © AP/Wide World Photos;
28-29 Girl Sneezing © A. Davidhazy/Custom Medical Stock Photo; 32 Radhakant
Bajpai courtesy of Guinness World Records; 34 Ram Singh Chauhan © Sherwin
Crasto/AP Wide World Photos; 35 Shamsher Singh courtesy of Guinness World
Records; 36-37 Ramos Gomez Brothers © Rex Features; 40 Monte Pierce courtesy
of Fox Broadcasting; 43 Kimberly Goodman © Drew Gardner/Guinness World
Records; 44-45 Rob Williams © Brenda Ladd Photography/www.brendaladdphoto.
com; 45 Watermelon © Peter Neumann via SODA; 46 Pierre Beauchemin © Michel
Bontemp/PONOPRESSE; 49 Ghosted Tomato © Bob Doctor/Morguefile; 50 Wedding
Rings © Photodisc via SODA; 51 Fire Breathers © Toby Melville/Reuters; 52 Slimed
Stars © Fred Prouser/Reuters/Landov; 53 Tomato © Dean Perry/Morguefile;
54-55 Garlic Festival © Marcio Jose Sanchez/AP Wide World Photos; 58 Bog
Snorkeling © David Jones, PA/AP Wide World Photos; 59 Darren Lott © Dave Auld/
www.auldovertheroad.com; 60 Wife Carrying © Tommi Korpihalla/EPA/Landov; 61
Toes © Malinda Welte/Morguefile; 63 Pachyderm Polo © Sam Tinson/Rex Features;
66 Around the World in Eighty Days © Everett Collection; 67 Bat © Photodisc via
SODA; 68 Prairie Dogs © Kenneth M. Highfill/Photo Researchers, Inc.; 69 Woodland
Frog © John M.Burnley/Photo Researchers, Inc.; 70 Gorilla Nest © Rodrique Ngowi/
AP Wide World Photos; 71 Bald Eagle © Photodisc via SODA; 74 Spiderwebs, 78
Polyphemus Moth Caterpillar © Anthony Bannister, Gallo Images/CORBIS; 75 Wasp
Nest courtesy of Guinness World Records; 76-77 Cockroach Racing © AFP/Getty
Images; 79 Ant Map courtesy of Laurent Keller; 83 Largest Shoes © Romeo Ranoco/
Reuters/CORBIS; 84 Biggest Flower © Frans Lanting/Minden Pictures; 85 Sperm
Whale © Francois Gohier/Photo Researchers, Inc.; 86-87 Elephant Orchestra © Jason
Reed/Reuters/Landov.